No Elegies

D1738619

No Elegies

poems

Lindsay Wilson

QUERCUS REVIEW PRESS
MODESTO, CA
2015

QUERCUS REVIEW PRESS POETRY SERIES
Sam Pierstorff, *Editor*

Published by Quercus Review Press
Department of English
Modesto Junior College
quercusreviewpress.com

Cover photo by Harry Wilson
Author photo by Anna Wilson

Printed on acid-free paper
10 9 8 7 6 5 4 3 2 1

Requests for permissions to make copies of any part of this work should be mailed to: Permissions, Quercus Review Press, Modesto Jr. College, 435 College Avenue, Modesto, CA 95350

ISBN-13: 978-0692366189
ISBN-10: 0692366180

Publications by Quercus Review Press (QRP) are made possible with the support of the English Department at Modesto-Junior College. A portion of the proceeds from the sale of this book will benefit creative writing scholarships at Modesto Junior College.

CONTENTS

IV.

There there now, Nothing.
Stop your sniveling.
—Larry Levis

Each animal makes his own wisdom.
—Lee McCarthy

No Elegies

Your therapist banned the word elegy
from your notebooks, by therapist I mean

the woman who runs your poetry workshop
at the food court in the high-end fashion mall

where apparently no one dies. Elegy is so,
what's the year Levis passed? Yeah, then.

No one said the sale would last forever,
and anyway, lately, haven't you been confusing

your favorite literary magazine for a sales
catalog? Doesn't your therapist say,

You shouldn't make everything into a poem.
Usually you're halfway up the drive before

you realize you're reading ad copy
instead of a haiku sequence. Haiku? Who do you

think you are? Basho? Hass? McGrath?
No, you're the odd boy standing

in your kitchen gazing out the window
where the whole world's a giant no.

The beautiful daisies half in fence shadow?
Old fashioned. The stark morning moon?

Are you being ironic? Your father's old
push mower leaning against a wall? A tool

from another century. You can't help loving
the transience. The waning moon. The flowers

that only love for a season. The rust dulling
the blades. Don't you love the Once of backstory,

or objects suddenly aglow, lit from within
by the human gaze? You were the boy who knew

all the lyrics from your parents' old records,
and you settled didn't you? Settled

for the teaching gig full of missed allegory,
settled for Saturdays spent in the food court

where your therapist puzzles and moans over
your new poem's ending: Once you stood before

the turned earth of the dead, and you thought
it the shape of a door, but without a handle,

so how do you enter without a lock to pick?
At lunch on the patio, a man pulled a dove

from his sleeve, and he let you touch it to make
it real for everyone else, and in one toss you saw

the bird become action, become flight,
and in that just-past-your-reach moment

your father said, *Don't worry. He's trained
to fly back to his cage.* Like a heart, you thought,

but said, *Don't ruin it.* You felt defiant in your grief.
At least then you could tell the world, as it drifted

below you, how you felt, how you could feel your hollow
boned lightness, how you could feel the hinges

of your wings pivot on the wind.

I.

Mother Seen as a Dress on a Line

After so many summers of fire you found
yourself complaining all through a green July,

and by the time you flip the calendar's page,
you're deep into a late August day

walking the dog between the freckles of low
pines when you both hear the owl's song,

a call without a body, carrying across
the creosote field where someone

in the distance beats a rug hung from a line,
and with each swing something old rises

briefly into the air, drifting in sun
and wind that distorts and billows, at the end

of the line, a long white dress into a body,
into something almost human. At home

the phone's ringing. It's been ringing all day,
and you're the only child, who walks

now with your mind wrestling with the dress
lifting for the wind. The world's calling.

Everyone wants to know the Story of How.
So how does it feel, this life, this evening

walk with your dog up a dry hill, knowing
there's no longer a woman to call, *Mother?*

Mother,

I'm tired of reading
the signs like a neighbor
balancing the weight
of three newspapers
on the drive,
                tired
of the way the plant's
dry soil tells him how long
it has been kept from water.

Bakersfield now is always August
with its wide open mouth trying
to get everything inside:

all those aphids devouring
the roses and the tarantula
wasps like the past trying
to put the weight of its eggs
in our backs.

                There are too
many things for our gaze
to fall upon, and misread
like a sign, so I've packed
up the car and written
this note, but where now
to send it?

Ars Poetica

When the police broke through the backdoor,
the window fell in pieces like the start of a story,

something in the middle of things, or already
at the end, depending on how the pieces are picked up

and arranged. Either way they must be gathered,
this trail of crumbed glass, this crumbled line

from backdoor to the back bedroom, this path the police
took to her body past the restored radio her father

cobbled together from the parts of old radios
no one ever listens to anymore, those radios

that must warm up before telling their who-done-its,
that refinished wood hiding the tubes inside.

The tubes, she told her son as a child, still held
the voices of the past, something trapped,

and if he could tune it just so, there they suddenly
were, almost alive and speaking to him on his knees,

squinting his ears at the needle, hand on the knob.
Though he's no child now trying to hear those old voices,

there's no nothing dead-alive in those tubes
despite all the antique frequencies no one listens

to anymore, not even the police, not even him,
or the coroner who followed the glass to her,

who took note of how she broke her nose, falling
in her last steps, the small halo there of dried blood,

the temperature of the body, how she knelt
over her and slipped off her wedding ring

to place in the jewelry case by the antique Czech
glass earrings he bought her. He gave the band

to his stepfather, gave the earrings to his fiancée,
and when he gathered the broken glass on the carpet,

it was almost beautiful, almost something to be hung
from sterling silver, then an ear, beautiful there to catch

the light for his eyes so it would lead back to what hears
his story. Her listening. Her ears adorned

with the antique glass she always wore when she knew
his eyes and her would be meeting.

How I Learned to Lie

If I want people to think
I'm not an asshole, I give them
the chair my book bag uses at coffee shops.
If the coffee shop's owner asks
what I think of his out-of-focus
black and white photos with hairs and dust
on the prints, I say nothing
about the overrated reputation of Ansel Adams
or my fear of underexposed gray landscapes
with poor depths of field matted under glass.
You could ruin a family dinner
by telling my father you love his teacher,
Ansel Adams, because you don't know
any photographers, and you want
to sound intelligent by stating the name
on the poster of aspens you bought at the mall
to hang by your toilet. The aunts will cringe,
and the pomegranates in the salad
will turn to bloody teeth
as you wait for his rant to begin.
I confess I don't appreciate Caffè Americanos,
photos of meadows, and small talk
with people who feel so much
for blurry captured light
they decided it's even better framed,
displayed and given a price tag of several
founding fathers. If I've learned anything
from my many meals of broken teeth,
and the hours I spent in my father's dark room,
it's that not everyone should own a camera
and art's as hard as lying to them is easy.

Consolation Prizes

A good dog that died young; dozens of purple-black bruised eyes;
days lost staring off the edge of a pier, my lines breaking in the sea

as the scales of silver fish flashed the sunlight like knives;
all those nights I spun funky house music at the Parlor bar for free;

my divorced parents' wedding gift plates, silverware, their old bed;
all the mirrors that cut off my head, my height, my bad knee's strain;

one ex-fiancée and all the meaningless threats of suicide she said;
notes from my scratched record of Coltrane's *Blue Train*;

beautifully polluted Bakersfield sunsets casting long shadows;
my old-fashioned romantic love of distance on western highways;

happy hour's free beers; envelopes of those rare holiday photos;
a fractured, blue egg shell, Spring's song of scatter across red clay;

after midnight, a bent wedding ring found as I staggered home,
winking at me from street snow, cold metal, something thrown.

Long Division

Death divides us into those who can clean
the blood stains of family and those who cannot.

The coroner called it pooling, normal,
this dark troubled-spot by her bed,

but I named it place of her last misstep, thought,
and had no desire to clean it. For days

I walked past it, stepping over its threshold
as I entered the room to part the blackout

curtains covering the glass door to the patio,
but the light never seemed long enough

to reach it, wash it—even in the length
of evening it could not touch it. I took out

my measuring tape, a pencil, a small notebook,
a matter of inches. I thought perhaps

during one of June's long days the sun
could make it. I had plans, calendars

and almanacs, though, I always fail
at forethought and math, but on that shrinking

late September day, the sun stopped two
and a quarter inches from her blood. I know.

I measured twice. When I stretched out
next to it, almost my whole body aglow

in dusk-light, all the dead relatives
from their pictures seemed to watch.

I memorized the ages of all of them,
then divided by the distance between frames,

added the baby nephew before I subtracted
all the Baptist family in Dallas, and I understood

this is where it ends, Mother, alone and blue-lipped
on the stained carpet as the gathered dead

look down on us with all of those unblinking
eyes, all those still mouths, and that carefully

measured distance between us shrinking.

Religion

Watching those super eight movies
of learning to walk, it took only one

of my father's fingers to keep me up.
At seven, I felt, for the first time,

the impossible past behind me, and felt it again
on a day trip with him to his hometown,

Bodfish, California where no one lived
at the old company town. The tan houses

had faded into the tan hills like old photographs
exposed to sun. He stood looking

further into place than I could,
and because that town was all flint

and kindling, his lit eyes drew sparks
and started small fires to the dried gullies

of this memories. *Once*, he began,
because that was how he was taught

to begin a myth, *I buried my turtle
in a cigar box under this tree*. We did not pray,

but got down on our knees
digging our hands into the dry earth,

hoping for a box with an empty shell inside.
When the earth gave us nothing,

my only proof became his face and words,
so I took faith, for the first time, in my father,

in the way prayer always remains outside of me
like a father must as he trails off before ending

another one of his impossible stories.

What I Remember About Bakersfield College Football Games with My Father

We'd park on the hill above the stadium's glow,
so he could walk me past the glass blowers' glow.

We should always consider glass a liquid, he said,
while tongs formed the openings—the O of glow.

Let's say then my mouth shaped bottle or vase,
to fit his lineage: did I need to grow into the glow?

What remained of me in his shadow that could not shatter,
in his camera's captured light, all found in his photos' glow?

I can't forget us in his darkroom watching images
bloom on paper under the safe light's yellow glow.

Is this how myths grow: attention and light, training
our eyes, the passed-on desire to show the glow?

Victory's the night's slow-motion applause, while we
wear confetti's shattered snow bright beneath the glow.

Fathers, sons and football—the formation of some myths—
you need tongs, Lindsay, to touch, to know his glow.

The Day's Other Face

Because you haven't stopped in weeks
you still feel the constant rattle of road,

and even at dusk, when you finally try
to stop for the night's first beer

like your mother walking in from work
to pour that first glass of wine. No music.

No television. *No talking*, she'd say
as she sat staring off into nothing

and began to wrestle with whatever
of the day's voices she still had to reconcile

in her mind before the evening could roll over
to show her other face. Today you desire

anything you think will stop your family's questions,
but you cannot shake the highway's thrum

from your bones, and you understand
you're praying for the first time.

How dramatically stupid you feel in your bartering,
your shaky hands empty with nothing to offer,

but you find here a sort of relief,
and then the lamp by her ashes casts

its sudden spell of light into the dusky room,
and this rattled moment feels like a torch

dropping through some deep well before
going out, and then you remember you

put the lamp on a timer, so it would look
like someone was here when no one was home.

II.

The Girls I Keep Falling in Love With

They didn't mind being plural.
—Brenda Hillman

I'm Bonnie; you're Clyde, she says. Something fruity with an umbrella.
    She says,
Beer. She says, Round of shots. Tequila without the training wheels,
    please, she says.

She writes our names on afterglow car windows as the radio's song bleats
about addiction. She sparks a Camel. I need to quit these, she says.

She loves brass. Hates the blues. Believes Romeo and Juliet romantic.
She prefers oranges over apples. Prose over poetry. Provolone to Brie, she
    says.

She ties her hair back then picks at cold Moo Shoo pork with chopsticks.
"Luck is the fruit of hard work." I hate their fortune cookies, she says.

Sparking a Winston-Salem, she says, Your name again? (and then) I have
    to go.
I'll call you. You call me. Don't call me. Lindsay, you have to leave, she
    says.

Fields Almost Like Love

The sun on the ground here flickers like flames
burning across this patio, where birds peck

then look me in the eye. I wish I could live off
so little, crumbs and glances weighing

almost nothing, but I'd fail like light imitating fire.
The newspaper tells us the new death toll

and how the forest fire restarted with the help
of the high Sierra winds. You will arrive soon

with our little bird dog, who won't sit still for the birds'
taunts. Cayenne, little pepper of a dog,

sesame in her tail, licking at crumbs smelled
in the stirred piles of dead leaves and ashes

falling around us like snow and oddly beautiful.
But, what summer is this without rain?

And who hasn't set fire to the fields of their life
and seen the scorched earth's promise of renewal?

When you arrive, the radio will bleat
its purple wounds, as I press my face against you

and consider leaving your fields, elbow of a creek,
hill of a knee, your stomach's meadow,

where I will see the smoke veil and soften you
and cloud the ashen air almost like love.

Wasp in a Trap

What trick is this room with no escape,
this plastic cone hung from a branch?

The wasp followed the sweet scent
through the air's various tripwires,

and believed it found a heart, a host body?
Attraction is as natural as repulsion,

but what force keeps it crawling here,
an instinctual scent, or a trapdoor, a way out?

Because I haven't found my way out of a body
since birth, because you've taught me to see

all the world as a trap, I now understand
I crawl for your sweet lures, and that escape

from your plastic heart never flowered,
even briefly, within my insect mind.

All That's Left

She said easily in the hallway, *I'm leaving.*
Surrounded by white walls, I became what was left.

Above our apartment, for some air, I walked our dog.
The clouds erased the stars—only the tall moon was left.

I wanted a flight to a small town with a name harsh as wool,
where those of us who've escaped mauled are left.

I've traced the roads between here and the mountains,
plotted the fall, memorized the turns, a right, a left.

In the vacant lot on an old bed, a dog's leash, a map,
plastic flowers, a red ball tossed and left.

Believe me, I've understood her theft, and all
those words on my list labeled: *Why she left.*

I wrote my own: thieves and honor, drugs and recovery—
out of twelve steps, we had only two small ones left.

All your lists and words expose you, Lindsay,
as a fool—you are what the paltry thief has left.

Seek

All she wants is static with a road
under her. On clear nights, radio waves speak
all the way from Montana, the Dakotas, Colorado.
In between static, mixed voices.
Music, static. Talk, static. Commercials, static.
Well, Linda, we don't know because the good book
doesn't tell us, but it seems she was beaten
to be made fun of— Static. Finger on the seek button.
Numbers counting up by themselves.
Mileage and speedometer, the lighter's flick.
Pledge drive happening now. The phone lines are open—
Two fingers holding a wheel and a cigarette.
Metallic burst of brass, flare of trumpet,
the undercurrent of bass line, then—
The ease of cruising smooth pavement.
Jenny, listen, even a Seeing Eye dog wags its tail
at its owner, and so the Congress—
Gust of wind pushing the car to the shoulder.
Traffic report. Weather report. War report.
Inaudible pop song. Little white crosses
on the shoulder. Blue guitar rift. High hat.
hey, hey, hey— The cigarette's cherry bouncing,
signaling in the rearview mirror.
No one in America should have to apologize
for making a living— This is her black night.
Smoke curling out the window. Doesn't every
story have the fight or flight chapter?
Poor pop song in the dark. Poor painted face
on the glass hovering over the landscape.
Poor highway of few desires.
Cold coffee in the cup holder. His thumbprint's
bruise on her forearm. Her cut scars.
Shake off the cold, southern Wyoming—
It's all static. Nicotine, gasoline.

Sunglasses rattling on the dash.
High plains one-way, Rockies the other.
In her dreams the radio only hisses with no words
to memorize, just the trance of dashed lines
behind the ironic bobble-head Jesus.
No horizon. No moon. No past tense fogging
the glass. Just static. Seat reclined, the fast lane,
she's barely steering—in the distance, headlights.

Ghost Piano

She parts the curtains
to let the morning's sun spill
into her gray kitchen.

On the sill, he left her
five cigarettes, matches
by a dirty ashtray. She inhales

noticing onion on the tiles
like a fallen crescent of moon
while she scrapes butter across toast.

After a thorough sweeping,
she takes polish and rag to the staircase
she cleans on Tuesdays, humming

to Art Tatum's piano in her ear.
He doesn't like her listening alone
where the space by the sofa no longer

makes a sound, because it isn't there.
At dusk, she cuts onions
as close to the ends as possible

without slicing herself
then she fingers *Under a Blanket of Blue*
on the kitchen counter,

hands waltz next to the lazy boil,
until he arrives hungry,
with a new pack of smokes.

In his palm, he holds her flame,
and she considers onions softening

in the broth, and the empty space

where her piano used to sit
as her hands trail along his neck,
and he doesn't know she plays there

the last few notes of her song.

Three Ways to Paint the Side of a Boxcar

I. Train

Sometimes this tagger wishes to transcend his own life
like brakemen in the train yard stumbling
for the first time across a mural,
to feel what the viewer feels.

Sometimes he practices his tag on the air
with just his hand, the way Coltrane moved
fingers over keys without blowing into his horn,
until he can spray his name without thought
onto back alleys, mailboxes, trains.

He knows his art's roots: cave paintings made
using hollow bird bones filled with colored dust,
waiting for breath to blow it onto stone.

Because the caps control the spray's width,
he worries about them
like Coltrane worries about reeds—
wants neither the line or note
to bleed into something else.

The sketch of his next mural is Philadelphia, 1943,
where John plays alone, but he isn't Trane, yet.
Tired from refinery work, he practices his horn
in a third floor walk up, but that's not in the picture.
Instead, he blows a note wrong
and a shade of dissatisfaction crosses his face.
From a new reed, he'll trim the slightest shaving
before holding it against the light.
He wants the reed to vibrate perfectly
and imitate the shimmering legato
he loves in Hodges. He's still learning

to shape the music with his hands and mouth,
learning how his breath curves and escapes pure
like a painting leaving on a boxcar—
something made that can't be owned.

This evening the tagger places *Monk's Music*
on the record player, and when the jacket opens
a shower of green escapes. A clue
from his father, trapped in the plastic covering,
from some forgotten late night
where someone must have slurred,
Is this the one with Trane?

It burns as easily as the paper he rolls it in,
and the high casts him back to the seventies,
where he woke to horns and pianos
drifting on smoke. He tried to hear each note,
each muffled voice, until the night turned
its first shade of blue. This evening,
he stares at the album cover on his easel
and thinks this kind of blue is the obvious choice,
but he'll use it anyway,
along with other bright colors,
which look atonal, so tomorrow morning
the piece will look right from his viaduct perch,
and when it leaves, the straining metal will moan
through the wheel's clicks
as the ceaseless human traffic drowns
out the morning birdsong.

II. Restoration

For her, the moment happened
during a lunch rush, the shoulders of busboys,
plates appearing and disappearing
through the clamored traffic of waitresses
when the heavy, two-beat rumble

cuts through Laramie,
she felt the low rumbling in her feet,
then Coltrane flew by, playing his sax
on the side of a boxcar.

He captured the saxophonist blowing colors
so alive he seemed destined to fracture
under the strain, but the tagger gave him
such wild and elongated hands
she imagined them capable of holding back
any pain, and his eyes,
huge and luminous, cast a spell that stayed
just four beats, or two large window frames,
before he exited stage right.

Later her palms touched an entire gallery
of rusting canvases on stalled boxcars,
and when the flaking murals broke under her hands
her hatred of sun and wind began,
and now, when she finds them
shedding a skin of rust and paint,
she knows she must try to stop them from fading.

III. Alibi

Say I hung with the tagger in his Denver studio
listening to all the right jazz records
his father left as he slouched
into a chair and told me to the story
of Miles Davis in Detroit trying to quit junk.
Cliff Brown had invited him to play,
but he arrived in the middle of the set,
trumpet in a brown paper bag,
strolled up to the stage without apology
and played an awful version
of *My Funny Valentine*. Of course,
the tagger said, Miles denied it...said it was all lies,

41

but it's better to know the truth
and play the standards.

The truth is, if I've stood watch
while the tagger stole spray paint,
or watched while she restored murals
in the train yard at night,
it means I've loved every word they've said,
and I'm an accomplice to petty crimes.
making up stories for a painting
I saw on a boxcar late one evening,
rehearsing a mural of alibis.

Trumpet in a Pawnshop Window

Miles, tonight light's drawn to you
and Sonny in the park on 155th and St. Nicolas,
and it's just before the limits
of the three-minute 78 fell away,
so we see you as just a horn player on the verge—
thumbing a pawnshop ticket
and nodding at the high rises
blocking out the pock-marked moon.

In the space between you and that sky,
birds cling to electrical wires, but they are not
like notes on a staff. They've grown
as sick and thin from their addiction
to flight as you have,

and the light they briefly eclipse
from the high-rise windows
needles holes through the night
like a conductor punching tickets on a train.
But this is before you took the tracks home
to clean up, so it seems pointless
to wonder, when the birds throw their bodies
into that space, whether they fly toward some
thing or away from it.

The moon's just a scrap
to write notes across—not something
to believe in—it's only a paper moon,
thin and in danger of being blown away,
and you've grown used to playing
with borrowed trumpets,
and don't even own a horn,
just an unredeemed ticket that says so.

Eulogy for the Good Girl, Lee McCarthy

When Body my good
bright dog is dead

How will it be
to lie in the sky
without roof or door
and wind for an eye

—May Swenson, "Question"

All through the cavities of my house, the fan whirrs its white
noise. Television on mute as *the Miles Davis Quintet* fills my
Spartan rooms. I have four books open to a May poem. Lee
please call me tonight and say, *I know they both lack, but, Lindsay,*
which of these stanzas isn't the least? Save me from cheap noodles
and drinking another beer. I lived in Laramie and still couldn't
fall asleep. Did you sleep in Wyoming? Stepping off the bus with
son and suitcase, you only had two hands. You must have known
you found revision. Writing about highways, I cut out a line about
wind in your eyes—and its erasure. I cut another then write, *a*
Lee in need of a lee and hate it. I'm rereading Carver's poem about
NyQuil. Do I drive to the all night Safeway, or text someone
asleep? Work on that novel with the unlikable male protagonist?
No more NyQuil. No more grading papers. No more soccer in
the backyard with the dog, now afraid of the ball. No more trips
to the 24-hour diner for steak and eggs. No more Lee.

My friends are all on east coast time. My fiancée's asleep in Vegas,
and I'm in Nevada's dirty little secret watching infomercials in
TV's blue bubble and swearing that Pabst Blue Ribbon is non-
alcoholic. Even the guys at the halfway house next door are
sleeping. Even the dog knows this routine, my chewing without
hunger. You ordered, but didn't eat the first time we met, told
me you didn't wear seatbelts because they hurt your skin, handed
me a May Swenson poem asking, *What's my favorite line?* I wish I'd

said, *Lee, please eat.* Said, *Fuck, Cormac.* I wish for sleep, to forget
the shadows, the NyQuil, to quit filling in the dialog for every
commercial. When I change the channel, I swear *No Country for
Old Men* is on. I keep it on mute and watch him stash the money
under the trailer. He should have died on screen. I know, I know.
Something lives in absence, emptiness. But I just see an old man
failing to write a scene, my dog's sappy stare. I'm gazing back,
too. You snapped the best photo of my father and me I own. I'm
looking at your written words below the frame, thinking of you
absent from the photo. Dawn creeps in to point in a direction
I hadn't considered. The morning's a map—the promise of
distance—the white gap we loved between here and anywhere
else.

I don't yawn. Lee, I don't even sleep right, and I'll ruin the end
of this poem for you. I've revised myself as many times as you,
living hidden in most of the western states, failing at love. I want
to end this with praise, but I've driven too far into the distance,
talked too much, my old problem—the horizon forever receding.
You laughed the time I told you Miles Davis yelled at Coltrane
for not finishing his solo soon enough. Trane said, *But sometimes I
don't know how to end*, and Davis replied, *Take the fucking horn out of
your mouth*. You laughed genuine and dark, and it lifted from your
balcony, sure of itself, out into the Bakersfield heat, the valley,
deep into that good ole boy country, and then beyond.

III.

Surrender, A Prayer for my Mother

Listen, dark one, as the sun sets,

the Boxelder beetles come down
from the west wall to fly back

to their nymph tree, and in this late light

the long ash leaves look like the points
of bronze spears, dark and bloody

with the busy blush of the beetles' scarlet

wings. After the sun falls below
the Sierras, and the sundial becomes

useless under these lengthening shadows,

the fine-armed daughters of night
will sever your tether to this dim world,

then, dark one, you will no longer

be bound to this place. You will lay
down your spears. You will find

your red-black wings.

I Own Few Memories of Him

I enter them like driving into a covered bridge in a late May of ashes,
where the sudden darkness cloaks my body then erases his ashes.

When you're left with darkness pierced by holes the sun ate
through wood, how easy to forget a body, how easy to lose the weight of
      ashes.

The day my mother called with his final news I listened while she cried,
but I remember nothing she said until I heard her say, *His ashes*.

He taught me how to tie a hook on the bank of a slow, dirty river—red
and white bobbers, perch on a string—we used crickets for bait, not ashes.

On that shore nothing surfaced. We stared silently at a dusty curtain of elms
swaying on another shore. They never parted, but gave us ashes.

In the driver's seat, I mistook my mother's profile for his, and what
I believed to be lifting curtains were leaves the color of his gray ashes.

Where you spread him, Lindsay, you mistook the river's sound for locusts
eating the edges of a wind so slow you couldn't even pray it lifts his ashes.

Mother,

You did not need an invitation
to appear on the sidewalk at dusk,

so I took you out of my loss

and crushed you with the thistles
from the burned field then spread
across the doorways of my house.

Now, afraid to leave, I wander
the rooms asking the mirrors
if they too own a memory
of your reflection.
     They, like you,
stay silent.
     When the thunder speaks,
I open the windows to the hot house
and notice,
    for the first time,

how the backlit Sierras look
like a jagged cardiac line
pulsing against the horizon
before flat lining into the Great Basin,

and there you are again, outside
looking in, hand pressed to the screen

while the wind and rain pass through
a body that isn't there.

A Few Theories on Starlings and Dandelions

after Cornelius Eady

The dead spill and drift into the mold-black
earth and tug on the curtain of loss

as the wind stirs their ash-dust into a fist
that unclenches like a dandelion letting go

of its seeds. I have a theory about seeds
and loss and the small birds I've introduced

to live off both. I have theories I try
to forget about dandelions, words

and memories I try to pull out whole,
taproot and all. I have theories about herbicide

and the cultivation of non-native species
to eat the dead. I have knelt on the earth

with a trowel and let my digging say,
Don't come back. My theories aren't prayers,

aren't small birds with their low trajectories,
hunger and warbled-faulty song. The dead

have their mouths of ash, their flower-seeds,
the jagged tooth leaves of dandelions

that always come back waving their goddamn
yellow flags. I have a theory about growth,

about the color yellow, about the hair
and fingernails of the dead still inching out

past the moment of reaching. Are you a body?
Are you ash? Are you a box, a box of ash,

opened and spread thin and merging
with the earth like a seed taking its first step

to root, to growing under my skin like a song
I don't want to know the words for? And yet

I'm digging in, I'm singing hopelessly along.

Elegy with Lawn Gnome

Something grows under my grass at night,
poking its whitecaps out from the earth

in a fairy ring. In the window above it sits
the ashes of a woman I cannot bury,

and since she has lost her eyes
I hide a cracked, faded lawn gnome

leaning on a toadstool between the wild roses
tell him to report to me each morning,

but he just says, *Cottontail.* He says, *Blue jay.*
He says, *Nothing.* That's all he ever says,

and I confess I put those words in his mouth
because that's what I do when someone dies,

put my words into things, and ask them to speak
for me, but I don't want my words.

I want a new name for understanding,
more phrases for something lost.

My gardener names the ring's bare
earth center the dead zone. *But the dead*

zone, I say, *keeps growing like the swells*
of a blue stone dropped into a pond,

and the gnome and I are tired of the dead
growing in our yard. The gardener

doesn't trust the gnome, but tells me even
the dead zone eventually dies. At dusk

the gnome and I drink a few beers and stare
at the hole in our lawn where grass should be.

I'm sorry, I say, *for putting my words
in your mouth, sorry for my inheritance*

*of fungus, these white caps like toes
exposed from a shallow grave.*

The Night I Woke Up and Didn't See
the Neighborhood Burning Down

I understood you passed down your insomnia
after weeks of waking during the dead hour,

but sadness had snuck up behind me to place
its hands over my eyes. Had I opened my blinds

I would have noticed a world domed in a dark
orange glow, a tangle of flames up the hill,

and so blindness taught me its advantages
as I cupped water to my face, then studied

on my elm-skin hands my frayed and forked
lifeline that you carved into my palms,

mother, which is something like an inheritance,
this wooden myopia of self, all those leaves

I grew to cover my eyes. Soon I found
sleep, and the next day I awoke to a landscape

layered in ash, though, the night before
unknown to me, just blocks away, fathers woke

their kids from the smoky darkness of sleep,
placed them wrapped in the backseat, and once

they saw everyone was there, the mothers began
the old stories of flight, which always start

with smoke rising from under the door
as the hands of someone we love pulls us

out of ourselves to push us into a new world
where the rain drifting into our eyes is ash.

Black-Footed Country

I proposed fire as another form of growth
the morning we woke to find the field of sage

and creosote replaced by wind-stoked smoke
and burning bushes. My mother had recently passed,

so you thought I was speaking in metaphor,
but I said I was speaking in world. That evening

the clouds wrung from our hopes appeared
and rained the ash from the air, and I came back

to my mourning in this new black-footed
country where I still couldn't write that grief,

and yet I knew some dormant seeds need fire to grow.
Another metaphor, you said, *What do you want?*

I asked, *The smell of creosote after a desert rain?*
Can't have that, you said. *They were all consumed.*

So I wrote of the steam rising from the charcoal fields,
and how lost I felt watching the returned-evacuated

children's flashlights scatter across the ridgeline,
and in between their shrieks of laughter I thought,

Where are the mothers to lead them home?

Mother,

Today I rise early to walk
the dog along the river,

restless and looking for what
the world will give: half-filled jar

of salmon eggs, broken antler,
a tripwire fishing line I pull up

and follow to a landlocked pool,
filled by a spring flood, then abandoned,

destined, by early summer, to dry up.
At the sound of my feet a school

of minnows startles out of their stillness,
and when I drop in a pink egg, they return

like my grief under the netted shadows
of the cottonwoods, exposed

in their appetite. I am training
my grief to rise from the shallows

for each bright egg, but even after
the jar empties, all those little mouths

still blindly bite at the surface.

On the Limitations of Surrealism,
or My Dog's Dada Poem

This morning, after I took my dog to read
the lawn's daily news of scents,
and she left her letter-to-the-editor
in the grass, we climbed out of the heat
into our house's cool rooms, where we shook
ourselves and chased ice with our tongues.

My Shiba Inu doesn't bark, she screams
and whines, which means sometimes
she almost finds a word, and I begin
talking in my baby-doggy-voice, until,
I say, *Don't roll your eyes at me*,
and she leaves to chew through something.

Later, I find today's chew toy,
Literary Magazine of the Moment,
the top half shredded and scattered
across the carpet, which is when I chastise her
for not finishing the job. *I don't want
a lazy dog,* I scold, *you have to learn
to end what you begin, Cayenne,
there are literary principles involved*,
and then I find, among the brown lint,
her dada poem, while she stares
head down, almost reconsidering
the arrangement, as if she's been chewing
on my *Surrealist Party Games* in her spare time,
and I read from my knees:

always broken
                    sand
a you   in reason

floating the unopened

fabric listeners
sleek maybe
          smoke
                    clouds

pools clasped
upon   a vibration

IV.

What Memory Wants

The moths, those little white flames
of evening, have grown tired of beating

their chapped wings against the streetlights,
and have silenced themselves into the leaves

along your porch where this morning,
in my sleeplessness, I imagine you robed,

kneeling down to clip rosemary
to bake later with chicken and the juice

of two lemons already resting on the table
with your coffee. Mother, did you notice

the new owner removed the shrubs
we planted along the fence line and dug up

the succulents from the porch's shade?
Mother, we showed him the room in which

you passed, and too early I am awake
with the guilt of selling that ground

because if the importance of place
are the acts committed to memory there,

then I am ashamed this morning has pressed
the gold coins of nostalgia to my palms

letting me see you in the kitchen,
garlic and rosemary on the counter

as you juice a lemon while the flames
of yellow finches darting from your wrists

and into memory's want, rise into the high branches
to grow fat like a sour fruit, and remain far

from our reach where they belong.

Falling Through a Telescope

When you look through a telescope
you see back in time through the light's
journey from itself to you, my mother explained
reclining in her lawn chair, the summer
she declared even some of the stars spinning
in their orbits had already died, and as my stepfather
grilled chicken, she sipped tea.
Mother loved teaching the names and how to gaze
back like a witness.
                   She sprinkled sugar
into her tea the way, she said, snow fell
on Bakersfield in March the day after I was born,
and that's how the impossible occurs—too sweetly.
A mother wakes to find her son transfixed
by snow drifting past the hospital window
and begins to write the story of why
her son always feels like snow is an open
cell door leading to an escape that doesn't end
in striped light.
              Pardon all the sugar.
My mother hated astronomy and preferred wine
with dinner because it made her forget
what she didn't remember. We never owned
a telescope. She would be the first to correct
my perjury, that I don't even know
how to look through the lens of our past,
besides, most nights in Bakersfield
you can't see through the smog. But I see
those nights still circling, and me there, spinning
and spinning in the backyard until I felt sick
and fell down as the adults did, eyes rolling over
to find the vault empty, no past falling on me,
and no clouds releasing their acquittal of snow.

Christmas Eve 2011 After Taking Yu Troung to Radiation, Christmas Eve 2012 After Learning He Passed

The worst thing about death must be the first night.
—Juan Ramon Jimenez

Snow drifts through the dark
then porch light before settling

into the bucket I used to mix soil
with manure to spread with seed

across my lawn where now snow grows,
flake by flake, slowly the way

a blues song enters us note by note,
or the way I imagine radiation

entered your body drip by accumulating
drip until your body said enough,

and on the drive home you gave it all
back to the bucket you kept at your feet

then carried to the porch to set down
like an afterthought, though, I never

wanted you to become an afterthought,
a bucket your wife hosed out, something

we used to beat like a drum
to keep us in time. Later it filled

with the accumulation of sprinkler and rain,
and I had a thought then I let pass,

an image really, of you on your porch
late that night, sleepless as I am now,

pencil in hand, harmonica in yours,
and when you peered down into the reflection

of your thin, sunken face did you see
our mothers looking down from their dark

windows above us telling us to sleep?
Because I can't. Though I know tonight

when the snow comes down like a curtain
on the sky, it means the moment

for all of those afterthoughts has passed,
it means it's time to play, to hold those notes

you love most rough and ragged
in your mouth because you'll have to sing

yourself to sleep, you'll have to practice
to turn your body into song.

The Sun to Worry

Twelve degrees this morning, and the pine trees
so full of ripe, dry snow that even though
the sky owns not one blemish of cloud
it still seems,
                    under these trees shoveling away
last night's storm, to be snowing down on me
with each gust of wind. The shadows will move
and allow the day's slim heat time to melt free
the road, the driveway, the path to my door.

If you start to sweat, I can hear my grandpa
say to my father, *slow down. You'll freeze up
if you get wet.*
                  These storms make us drive slow,
walk slow, dig, breath, think. My father
did this chore all through high school
in the southern Sierras before his father drove
to work, and now drives to the store because his father
cannot, fixes soup and salad, helps him walk, remember.

If I imagine the mind as a road we travel
through countries and cities,
                        my grandpa's dementia
has been driving him slowly back to Montana
where now the farm houses and lights in the distance
begin to click shut and the storm
taking down all the stars from the sky
has given so much snow the wind drifting there
begins its gradual, cold erasure of his road,
freezing it over, which is hard and slippery like memory.

Today, because I work tomorrow,
I break small gauges through the ice on my street.

I want some place, some small lesion,
where the sun can worry and begin to bring it all back.

Flight

Two backlit bodies meet in the distant apartment hallway
as you watch from icy-wet hills—so all the specifics

hide in framed-silhouette before you look down at the tracks
you've been following—footsteps in mud—each ripple

leaving its own pond in the night. Why did they stop
so suddenly? What's the last step in the far regions of loss?

And they finally came apart, the bodies that is,
as you knew they must. And the boot prints?

They stopped like the geese prints you found this morning
on the hillside, which end as suddenly as flight.

Your poor bird dog's nose confused, as she lifted her head
and sniffed the air for the steps from which they flew.

April in Laramie

I thought if I recited the stories again, followed our old flight to Laramie,
I'd find the door you stand behind, and, tonight, you'd let me in, Laramie.

I remember spring snows throwing their white rags across the prairie,
how we had to shield our eyes from all the bright light in Laramie.

Since then, I've walked past our old apartments, the abandoned depot, but still
I couldn't find her footsteps in snow leading back to her spite in Laramie.

At first we laughed through all our pasts' black eyes and scars,
and drunk on the Buckhorn's barstools we found delight in Laramie.

I used to think if the Big Sky showed a path, a road, from Star A
to Star B, I might then be able to hitchhike back to her in Laramie.

I've found the Oregon Trail, the Transatlantic Railroad, found I-80,
and all of their cuts through the high plains met right here in Laramie.

Despite our carved names in wood at the Buckhorn, despite the bullet hole
above the bar, none of these lead to our old plight here in Laramie.

Smoking in the snow she said, *We must remember flight has two meanings.*
How long before she realized it might have more in Laramie?

Even with all the names and landmarks, even with all your searching,
Lindsay, you will never find the sight of her ghost here, again, in Laramie.

Burying Bird Dog

for Cayenne

My ex-girlfriend and I took turns with the shovel
and gathering rocks from the river's shore.

When we finally sat, leaning against each other,
the unleashed wind blew between us

into the high-bone grass flushing a murmur
of starlings from the brush. It wasn't the first

time we understood we didn't know how to pray,
but after carrying the heavy stones

to cover her grave, we could feel her phantom
weight in our hands.

Elegy with no Shotgun

After everyone left me alone in her house,
I searched her closet first filled with sundresses
the smell of old, floral perfume,

then mine, empty and dusty for years,
and the guest bedroom and the next,
through the hallway closets and into the garage

with its corners filled with boxes and tools,
but still no gun oil, no wooden handle.
Not even in the black widow shed

could I find my old 410 overlay,
but finally beside the lawn mower
with its litter of dry, cut grass, I cleared away

a space in my mind and remembered
after her last failed suicide my father,
her long-ago ex, whose custody the state

so embarrassingly placed her in,
had taken it with others to be destroyed.
The gravel floor crunched like gritting teeth

as I ran to her car and sped off into the Sierra
foothills for any road to announce itself,
to say left here, right there. What the fuck

did direction matter? I wanted speed
under me. I needed a dirt road, more gravel
and a sun to come down hard on every damn thing

at some dead end. Some failed oil field lease.
Some collapsed homestead. Some place
to be in the world's teeth and chewed

until screaming took me, until only shooting
would do for the I-want-holes-in-everything mood
I was in. What do you give such hungry

and empty hands? So you've heard
this story. So your cynicism eats at you
like the bullet holes rusting through this fallen,

corrugated roof. Say, so what. Say who cares.
Say death sleeps in every one's bed.
What is it to you that once, as a boy,

I shot at clay pigeons and the ground
broke everyone? So she took me out from under
the gaze of the men who laughed

with each of my shots. Quail sprung from sage,
ran through the red rocks, and vanished
into the yellow bloom of rabbit brush.

She said, *Easy, relax.* She said, *Try again.*
But my anger swelled with everything I missed.
Once there was patience, a mother and son

alone, and the perfect complete arch of clay pigeons
that must break when finally their flight
takes them back to this hard, dry earth.

Landscape with Two Young Poets Fishing
for Ben Gotschall

The uncanny sense that the landscape is looking back at us.
—Willard Spieglman

We were bored fishing the stiff
sheet of the August reservoir.

When we cast our lines
to the edge of the still lagoon,

did we drag our small grappling hooks
through the algae-thickened lake

to see if sight itself left its mark
across the land? What did we find

except our eyes staring up at us
from the wind-wrinkled surface,

the awkward floating pier that rose
and dipped when the waves said so,

another's old hooks and broken lines,
minnows, leaves, rust?

I caught something then with just a glance.
Meeting the reservoir half way, I said,

I'm a body of water too. I know
what I felt when that chance pack of coyotes

howled so close, my hands shook
and stopped their reeling in, letting

the lure drop and snag in weeds.
We foolishly believed then

in howling back, dancing
and running back to shore,

that each yip and yell
was a call, was meant for us.

Slip

Who could say how long you stared
out past her fence line through a field

of tumbleweeds and foxtails,
where an oil pump bowed mindlessly

through the late summer heat?
But grief is a drug, a hunger

that makes you gaze out at the world
hoping to see more than you know,

like staring at old photographs
of her and asking meaning to appear

as suddenly as a kit fox in the field,
something quick-small, the color of dry grass,

that you hadn't noticed. And somehow
the world confirms your need,

but you're too old to believe this now,
because all the world gives today

are the oil pump's gears chewing
through the brutal Bakersfield heat,

which is enough to make you strip bare
then slip into the pool's cool throat,

eyes closed as you slide just under
the surface, hoping to be swallowed whole.

No Revision

This evening, as a tiding of magpies perch too loudly
in the low pines, I reread the last pages from the history book

of the correspondence between my mother and I, my fifth
beer sweating onto my grandfather's oak table. If you read

this scrapbook of knee-jerk letters and cards glued to the pages,
some blank, some torn out, you'd find at the end the first draft

of Bishop's "One Art" next to the final draft that I sent
after a woman my mother knew insisted, *You cannot revise*

poetry. It's too personal. She called too late that night,
and in between gulps of wine, I heard her familiar near manic

voice, the long pauses as she measured each syllable,
each nuance of word before speaking too carefully,

before finally saying, exasperated, *Isn't that crazy?*
Tonight, I've winched up her manic voice into the trees

to let it carry between the two poles of me, east to west.
The magpies, their calls sharp and angry, now fight

in the road over a truck-hit coyote. My bird dog whines
at the fence line. *No, you're not crazy, Mother*, I wrote

on the drafts of Bishop's poem before sending my last note.
The day she died, I spoke with the coroner on the phone

about her depression, suicide attempts, and Lupus' beak
picking at her old heart. She asked, *Would your stepfather?*

No, I said. And then suddenly she said, *What do you do?*
I try to teach writing. She asked, *You recently sent poems?*

And I saw her in my mother's room, this lady whose job
deals with the art of losing daily. They had already

carried my mother out under the feathered shadows
of trees and inside the coroner read "One Art" thinking,

No, shit. The art of losing isn't hard to master.
On the road, the magpies pick from the coyote's torn stomach,

and so scavenger eats scavenger, and the entrails spill out,
pulled from beak to bloody beak, then they carve their jagged

lines across the liver. Lines I read later, my dog straining
at her leash as the birds screech from the bouldered hill.

I can't predict the future. I can't read the scars on my liver.
I don't know what long history the coroner found inside her,

but I wanted to tell her how terribly we ended, still fighting
over my name on a failed suicide note without apology

and no way now to revise. I wanted to know what the coroner
found when she read the lines scarring her liver. Did she discover

I was an awful son? Maybe some things are too personal.
Maybe language never means what we desire so revising

is meaningless, and in some wrong way that lady was right.
But what do I know? I only revise my words on the page

and never my life. Maybe the coroner sat there flipping
between the first and final drafts thinking about the day's

new loss, and understood, for the first time, the art of losing
is hard to master. Tonight that thought lifts like a tiding

of black and white birds rising from a boulder strewn hillside,
and for a second they hold there, blocking out a few early stars,

and revise the bright blemishes from the evening sky.

Changing Your Name

At the coffee shop I wanted to photograph
a poem to text to you because I knew

you were in the Social Security waiting room
filling out the paperwork they make you gather

to change your last name to mine, and I thought
the poem would make you smile in a place

smiling is banned. How does it feel waking up
knowing your name is different from yesterday?

The strange sensation of holding a pen
and not knowing how to sign? I played

"Yesterday" at a recital when I was young.
Back then my mother taught me to read music,

taught me how a woman changes names
like a song shifting tone. When my mother

died, I sat before the old, walnut piano,
spread the sheet music I used to be able to play

in front of me and sat there silently
with the memory of knowing how to read.

How many selves had I tried on since then,
since I could transform signs on a page

into music in the air? Though I still held
a faraway memory of tight, fine clothes,

a low-lit room full of adults already fading
into their shadows, keys against fingers,

foot pumping its pedal, the absence of missed notes,
then the memory of applause. How many

yesterdays must fall faraway before
you're signing your name under the flickering

fluorescents of some dull waiting room,
and then when you look down at your name,

you think, how could I write this any other way?

Mother,

How many years did you try
to skip to the end?

You ripped out whole passages
took a permanent marker

to black out words
and phrases, erased your notes

in the margins.
                          I trace

my fingers over the pen's
indentations, try to discover

a letter, a new association.
Since birth you taught me

to read with my eyes shut,
how words rise in my mind

like lupus and low pines,
heat and transience.

You Only Half Understand,
or Hangover, Zancudo, Costa Rica
for Nick George

A loud wind this morning wakes you
from the dream in which she sits deliriously
penning a failed suicide note in the idling car
as you run from door to locked door.

She places the note on the dash, revs the engine,
and suddenly it's the sound of the rushing
high desert wind, the messenger of flame
and scorched earth, and yet the room's wrong,
the bed hard, the television small with a flood
of emotional Spanish you only half understand.

Outside the world calms before you hear
a loud thud, then another, and a deep-low knock
begins to ring. A friend steps from the kitchen.
Coconut water, he says, *Tico hangover cure.*

It's been years since you've seen him, since
she swallowed a bottle of pills and started
her car to drive nowhere. Is it possible
what you hold is a kind of gratitude, solace
given shape by a glass? Is there a cure?

Somewhere underneath your skin comes a ringing,
something broken from a hard skull, a shell,
a husk peeled back then discarded by the machete
half buried in sand, and when the next thud
comes close, rippling low and deep, you startle.

Your friend puts his hand on your shoulder.
*The coconut palms have been doing that all
morning,* he says, *bending in the wind,
then letting go, and then letting go again.*

ACKNOWLEDGEMENTS

I would like to thank my teachers Alyson Hagy, Paisley Rekdal, Mary Clearman Blew, Kim Barnes, and Robert Wrigley for all of their patience and time, and I would like to thank the Truckee Meadows Community College English department. This book could not have been written without my time spent at the Centrum Writers' Conference, so I would like to thank Jordan Hartt, Erin Belieu, Gary Copeland Lilley, Sam Ligon, Philip Shaw and the rest of my Port Townsend tribe. A big thank you to Eric Neuenfeldt, Susan Deer Cloud and Joe Wilkins. Thanks to Waldens Coffee shop for keeping me caffeinated and fed. For my Reno writing group I would like to say thank you to Ann Keniston, Steve Gehrke, Karen Terry, and Laura Wetherington. Big love to my father and the rest of my family, and to my wife, Anna Wilson, who loves me in spite of myself.

Grateful acknowledgement is made to the following publications in which these poems first appeared:

"Elegy with Lawn Gnome" and "Mother Seen as Dress on a Line" are forthcoming from *Clerestory*.

"Ghost Piano" was published under the title, "Under a Silent Blue Song," by *Pank*.

"On the Limitations of Surrealism, or my Dog's Dada Poem" was published in the *Portland Review*.

"Falling Through a Telescope" was published in the *Chaffin Journal*.

"Trumpet in a Pawnshop Window" and "Consolation Prizes" were published in the *South Dakota Review*.

"Three Ways to Paint the Side of a Boxcar" was published in the *Santa Clara Review*.

"I Own an Early Memory of Him" was published in the *Hiram Poetry Review*.

"How I Learned to Lie" was published in the *American Poetry Journal*.

"Fields Almost Like Love" was published in *Fogged Clarity*.

"All That's Left" was published in *Salamander*.

"Wasp in a Trap" was published in *Harpur Palate* and *Verse Daily*.

"Flight" was published in *Limestone*.

"The Girls I Keep Falling in Love With" and "The Sun to Worry" were published in the *Yemassee Journal*.

"Burying Bird Dog" was published in the *Clackamas Literary Review*.

"Eulogy for a Good Girl, Lee McCarthy," "Religion," and "April in Laramie" were published in the *Open Window Review*.

"Black-Footed Country" and "Seek" were published in the *Minnesota Review*.

"Elegy with No Shotgun" was published by the *New Plains Review*.

"Christmas Eve 2011 After Taking Yu Troung to Radiation, Christmas Eve 2012 After Learning He Passed" was published in the *Naugatuck River Review*.

"Mother, You Did Not Need..." and "Slip" were published in the *Cumberland River Review*.

"Surrender, A Prayer for my Mother" was published in the *Bellevue Literary Review*.

"A Few Theories on Starlings and Dandelions" was published by *Compose*.

"Mother, Today I Rise Early..." was published by *Sundog Lit*.

ABOUT THE AUTHOR

Lindsay Wilson, an English professor at Truckee Meadows Community College, has been a finalist for the Philip Levine Prize, and he has published five chapbooks. He co-edits *The Meadow*, and his poetry has appeared in *The Minnesota Review, Verse Daily, The Portland Review, Pank,* and *The Bellevue Literary Review,* among others.

Made in the USA
Charleston, SC
02 April 2015